"We must build dikes
of courage to hold back
the flood of fear."

–Dr. Martin Luther King Jr.

Praise for *You Can't Celebrate That!*

A beautifully written teacher's story about what it takes to provide children with the tools to act with empathy, respect, and fairness in the face of diversity.

~*Louise Derman Sparks and Julie Olsen Edwards,* co-authors,
 Anti-bias Education for Young Children and Ourselves

You Can't Celebrate That! is an intriguing and gentle love story from a teacher to her community.

~*Shoshana A. Brown,* LMSW, Educator, Organizer, and Healer

This book is just what early childhood educators need right now to understand our own racial and cultural biases, and to move forward to transformative teaching and learning.

~*Daniel Meier,* Professor of Elementary Education,
 San Francisco State University

Nadia approaches her teaching with a set of values as her steady friend and guidepost and is a model to all of us, showing how true humility, honesty and openness can build bridges with families and co-workers and provide fertile soil for anti-bias education to blossom.

~*Julie Bisson,* Early Childhood Director and author of *Celebrate!*
 An Anti-Bias Guide to Including Holidays in Early Childhood Programs

This book makes a compelling case for how the Aotearoa (New Zealand) approach to Learning Stories can help early childhood educators in the United States amplify the voices of children and provide a compassionate and practical way to connect family and community to the life of the classroom.

~*Barbara Henderson,* Professor of Education,
 San Francisco State University

You Can't Celebrate That! reinforces how important it is that we begin talking with children about race and racism at a young age. If it is our mission to prepare our students to live and succeed in our diverse and globalized world, our work begins here with intentional teaching about inclusion, equity, and identity.

~*Gab Sussman,* Seeking Educational Equity and Diversity (SEED)
 Facilitator and Elementary School Teacher

You Can't Celebrate That!

Navigating the Deep Waters of Social Justice Teaching

By Nadia Jaboneta

Edited by Ann Pelo and Margie Carter

ISBN 978-0-942702-98-9
eISBN 978-0-942702-68-2

Printed in the United States.

© Dimensions Educational Research Foundation, 2019

Book Design: Stacy Hawthorne
Editors: Ann Pelo and Margie Carter
Managing Editor: Tina Reeble
Production and Copy Editor: Emily Rose

Typeset in Adobe Handwriting / Frank and
Ivy Journal typefaces.

Photographs provided by Nadia Jaboneta.

The infographic *"They're Not Too Young to Talk about Race"*
is used by permission of The Children's Community School.
© 2018.

For more information about other Exchange Press publications
and resources for directors and teachers, contact:

Exchange Press
7700 A Street
Lincoln, NE 68510
(800) 221-2864 • ExchangePress.com

To my children, Ari and Leelah, who inspire me
every day and who make this world a better place!

With love, your Mom,

Nadia

A Call to Reimagine Our Work

The stories in the *Reimagining Our Work* (ROW) collection are anchored in the conviction that another world is possible for early childhood education—a world characterized by open-hearted and attentive collaborations between children and educators, in shared exploration of engaging ideas. This collection helps us begin to imagine that world, as we reimagine our work, moving beyond the joyless land of prescribed curricula with its corresponding outcomes and assessments, into the unpredictable, green-growing terrain of lively curiosity and rigorous critical thought.

Too often in our field, the discourse about educators reflects a diminished and disrespectful view of their capabilities for challenging, rigorous, generative thought. "Keep things simple and easily digestible," is a common caution. "Teachers want strategies that they can put immediately to use in their class-rooms. Don't offer too much theory, too much complexity."

We disagree. **Strongly.** We believe that educators hunger for deeper meaning in their work. We believe that educators long to be challenged into their biggest, deepest, most startling thinking and questioning. We believe that educators are ready to have their hearts cracked open and their imaginations ignited. We believe that educators are eager to explore how theory looks in everyday practice and how practice can inform theory. These convictions are at the heart of this collection of stories.

In these stories, children and educators take up ideas of substance, pursuing questions in ways that are unscripted and original. They braid fluid imagination and expansive awareness into their collaborative inquiry. The children in these stories aren't "gifted" or privileged—except by the gift and privilege of their educators' potent regard for their capability, and their concomitant willingness to bring their best minds and hearts to the table.

Which is just what we see the educators do in these stories. We hear educators reflect—in their unique voices and contexts—on their evolving understandings of children's capacities, and their roles as educators, and the meaning and practice of teaching and learning. The educators in these stories hold assumptions and visions different from the dominant paradigm in our field, and we have much to learn from them.

With the ROW collection, we hope to advance the conversation among early childhood educators, administrators, community college and university educators, policy makers and funders about the nature and practice of early education—a conversation which we also engage in the foundational book for this collection,

From Teaching to Thinking: A Pedagogy for Reimagining Our Work. As you read, we hope that you are challenged, exhilarated, unsettled, and rejuvenated. We hope that you find kinship in these stories. We hope that the stories in this collection carry your thinking far beyond curriculum ideas, and help you reimagine your work. May these stories sustain you as you stand strong with the children in your care. Resist the limitations of standardized curriculum, and claim, instead, the exhilaration of creating a new world, together with children.

—**Ann Pelo** and **Margie Carter**
  Editors of the *Reimagining Our Work* (ROW) Collection

  Authors of *From Teaching to Thinking: A Pedagogy for Reimagining Our Work*

For more information on the
ROW collection and upcoming titles
please visit ExchangePress.com/ROW

Contents

Foreword

We're never really ready for it, when it comes. As educators, we might have taken workshops, read case studies, practiced what we could say. But when it happens—the moment that calls us to integrate what we know and care about—we're caught off guard, left blinking, grasping for a response.

"You can't celebrate that! Only people with white skin can celebrate that! That's what my Dad said."

A simple, potent declaration, from one child to another. Skin color called out and used as a measure of belonging—or not. A parent's authority invoked to support race-based exclusion. One child positioned as gate-keeper. One child locked out.

We prepare for these moments in the hope that we won't feel unsteady and clumsy and tongue-tied and shaken. That we'll know just what to say, that we'll offer a smart, insightful comment that arises from our best thinking. But there's a darn good chance that we won't know exactly how to respond, that our hearts will race, our voices may catch, and we'll stammer. And in that moment, we have a choice to make: smooth things over quickly and steer the conversation in a more comfortable direction, or dive into a conversation about race and religion, about inclusion and exclusion, about identity and justice. Our choice has consequences not only for the children, but for ourselves.

In *You Can't Celebrate That!*, Nadia teaches us what's possible when we choose to join the conversation and learn alongside children. She writes about self-doubt and disequilibrium, *and* about her determination to say *something* that directly engages the fraught moment of exclusion—"Only people with white skin can celebrate that!"—and, importantly, to carry the conversation beyond that moment with the children. Nadia calls the children's parents, asking them to think with her about how to move forward; she talks with her colleagues and supervisors about what social justice teaching means in these real-time moments. Nadia's story of social justice learning at its most raw and unscripted is one of deep integrity—of alignment between her inner convictions and her behavior—and illustrates the risks, vulnerability, longings, and courage that come with such acts of integrity.

This is the teaching that Nadia offers us in her open-hearted, courageous story: when we engage with children and adults in real conversations about social justice issues—when we persevere, knowing that we don't have the perfect words, that our speech may be clumsy—we help shift our communities towards a full-hearted embrace of difference, of justice, of joyful welcome. When we feel exposed and shaky and awkward and unsure, we can take heart, recognizing our racing pulse as confirmation that this stuff matters, that it's the real deal.

All this takes courage, and a willingness to feel off-balance and unsure. It takes faith in a shared "longing to be part of real and transformative conversations, to stop living fearfully and cautiously around people who are different" (p. 81). It takes the conviction that all of us—children, families, teachers—deserve a learning community that is alive and generative and willing to engage in the strong work of social justice.

As Nadia's story unfolds, we see her change. Nourished by the relationships that grow with the children's parents, buoyed by her community of co-workers, Nadia becomes determined to watch for opportunities to take up issues of social justice with children—not just hoping to fumble her way to good-enough responses to children's comments, but actively to call forward conversations and explorations about difference, both with children and with adults. "I feel new muscles developing," she writes, "and I want to keep exercising them." (p. 77)

May this book inspire you to strengthen your capacity for social justice teaching and learning, exercising the muscles of courage, integrity, and empathy. Join the community of teachers, administrators, and parents working to create a more just, generous world. As the children in Nadia's preschool say, "We can spread kindness all the way to the White House! All over the Universe! To infinity!"

Ann Pelo and Margie Carter

Editors of the *Reimagining Our Work* (ROW) Collection

Authors of *From Teaching to Thinking: A Pedagogy for Reimagining Our Work*

Chapter One

Time Stops

This story of a startling and provocative conversation begins over a meal, as these sorts of conversations often do. I was eating lunch with the four- and five-year-old children in my preschool class, chatting about our day, when Harry, a mixed-race child, began to tell us about his evening plans:

*"I'm so excited for tonight!
I'm going to celebrate Shana Tova!"*

(his name for the Jewish holiday, Rosh Hashanah). "I'm going to eat apples and honey, and my Mom is going to read me my books about the celebration!" Harry's excitement was contagious. Children asked him questions about the holiday, and Harry had detailed answers. I noticed Kiley, a White child, looking at Harry for a long moment during the energetic conversation before she said, firmly,

*"You can't celebrate that! Only
people with white skin can celebrate
that! That's what my Dad said."*

My heart stopped. Kiley's comment came out of the blue, and landed with a heavy thud in the middle of the conversation. Harry looked surprised, confused. He got quiet and looked over at me. We had jumped from a cheerful, light-hearted conversation about holiday festivities into the deep waters of race and racism. My heart raced, even as it felt like time stopped for a moment. I had a decision to make. *How was I going to respond?*

I care deeply about addressing bias. I want children to know how valuable their differences are—to know that differences are what make us beautiful and unique humans. I knew I had to say something, *do* something. *But what? What could I offer that would ease the tension, support both Kiley and Harry, and get us out of this deep water?*

As I was grappling with how I should respond, I heard the voices of all sorts of people in my life who have influenced who I am. It was as though all of these people—including various aspects of myself—were standing on my shoulders giving me advice.

Me, Nadia, a Woman of Color

I first thought about why I was having this big reaction. My parents are both from Lima, Peru; they came to the United States 52 years ago so that they could have better opportunities for education, work, and raising a family. I was born and raised in San Francisco. I consider myself a Latina and a person of color. I went to an elementary school that was

predominantly White, without much ethnic diversity.
I have experienced feeling different than my peers and being
excluded because of my language, my culture, and the color
of my skin. I wanted to let Kiley know how hurtful her words
were. I wanted to tell Harry that I understood how he felt.

Me, Nadia, an Early Childhood Educator

I reminded myself that four- and five-year-old children
are beginning to develop stereotypes about themselves and
others, influenced by everything that they see around them.
I knew that Kiley did not want to hurt or exclude Harry.
Her intentions were to point out something she had
noticed based on her own experiences of being Jewish
and her observations of the Jewish people around her.

I thought of the dozens of anti-bias trainings and
workshops I had been to, and the anti-bias workshops
that I had facilitated with my colleague, Brian. During all
of these trainings, we'd explored how young children learn
about race. We practiced ways that we could respond to
children when comments about race or other differences
came up. But this wasn't a workshop; this was real life,
with real children with real feelings about their family and
cultural identities. I wasn't practicing now, and I wanted
to get it right. But here I was, at this crucial moment at the
lunch table, tongue tied from nervousness!

In the past, I might have redirected the conversation, wanting to get us all out of our discomfort and back onto easy ground. But I knew better now. I understood that silence can unintentionally reinforce stereotypes and can be hurtful. I knew in my gut and in my heart that I could not sidestep the issue this time. I imagined Harry going home that night, sad, his head bowed, telling his parents about what had happened at school that day. I could not let this happen.

How could I respond to show respect for both Kiley and Harry? I did not want my response to make Kiley feel like she was "in trouble" for her comment to Harry. But I did want her to know that it was not okay to exclude someone because of the color of their skin. I wanted her to know that she was in a safe place to make mistakes and learn from them. I wanted to reassure both of them that we were in this together!

The Voice of My Sister, Violeta

At a family gathering a few years ago, my sister told us about her five conversation rules. She said, "Never ask about finances, sexuality, politics, social standings, or religion." My family had a good laugh about these rules, but I knew she was not kidding. These five rules protect her from conflict with other adults. Conflicts arise from differences. Conflicts occur when people do not agree on their values. Conflicts can trigger strong feelings. These rules help her feel safe and secure. I could see why she abided by her five rules, especially in conversations with the strong-minded people in our family who have different experiences with and perspectives about these five topics.

While thinking about how to respond to Harry and Kiley—as well as what to model for the six other children at the lunch table—I thought about my sister's conversation rules. One of my most important jobs as a teacher is to provide an environment where children feel safe and secure. *How do I do that when conflicts arise about differences? Should these conversation rules apply to my work with young children?*

The Voices of My Executive Director, Belann, and My Fellow Lead Teachers

A few years ago, my colleague Brian and I helped plan a full day of professional learning about anti-bias curriculum for our staff. One session that we suggested focused on anti-bias books that we could read with young children, including Jacqueline Woodson's *The Other Side*, a story of the friendship between a Black girl and a White girl told in the context of the segregated South.[1] Brian and I felt that this poetic and poignant book would be a good way to spark discussions about race and racism.

When we met with the lead teachers and our Executive Director, Belann, to finalize plans for the workshop, we assumed that they would share our perspective about the book; the people on our staff are a progressive bunch, and Belann has been passionate and unwavering in her work to make our school community one that is diverse and inclusive. But our assumption that we all shared a similar perspective about the book was wrong.

Belann and several teachers voiced their concerns about exposing children to the violence and cruelty of segregation. Young children may not be able to make meaning of stories of racist segregation, they cautioned; they may well re-enact it—which had happened to a child dear to Belann, when her classmates heard historical stories from the Civil Rights movement. Some teachers argued that we should not expose children to hurtful and confusing concepts that could damage their self-image and their relationships with each other. Brian and I hadn't anticipated this—in fact, we hadn't thought of this point of view at all. We also wanted to keep the children safe from damaging ideas and images. We were stuck, all of us: *How might we move forward with our different perspectives?*

This meeting had really stuck with me. I thought of it often when I purchased children's books, planned curriculum, talked with colleagues, and interacted with children and families. I thought about it as I tried to figure out how I would respond to Harry and Kiley. I wanted to speak from my values, but I also wanted to honor the complexity of my co-workers' perspectives. *What should I say to Harry and Kiley that would take into account these varying perspectives?*

The Voice of My Dad, Enrique

I was raised in a typical Latino household, and respect was one of the most important values instilled in me. My dad taught me about a strong work ethic; being on time, working hard, being obedient to authority figures, and following the rules. These values helped shape who I am today. I have always been a rule follower, which can be a great asset. It can also be a challenge, getting in the way of self-reflection and critical thinking. As I considered how to respond to Kiley and Harry, I could feel the pull of my dad's teaching to "follow the rules." I didn't want to overstep my role or disrespect Belann's vision for our school community.

The Voice of My Colleague, Brian

While we don't teach in the same classroom, Brian and I have been thinking partners at our preschool for ten years. He's a White, gay man, and I trust him deeply; he's a person who I confide in and learn from. Although anti-bias education has always been at the heart of our work, in the last few years, we both have made this a top priority for our learning and teaching with children, families, and educators. We have studied research about the ways in which young children notice and think about race, and learned that *not* talking about race can reinforce racism. I wondered how Brian would advise me to respond to Kiley and Harry.

Safe, Secure, and Supported

My mind was swirling with all of these voices—and then I remembered a Learning Story that my friend and colleague, Keiko, wrote for her classroom about a conversation that she and our co-worker, Daniel, had with children about whether or not a boy can be an evil queen. During the conversation, Daniel affirmed that: "In this classroom, a boy can be a queen or king. A girl can be a king or queen. You can be whatever you want to be." And Keiko had underscored this message simply and strongly: "At Pacific Primary School, you can be whatever you want to be."

Daniel's and Keiko's statements inspired me and left me feeling safe, secure, and supported (and lucky to have such thoughtful colleagues!). This was how I wanted the children to feel: safe, secure, and supported. This was the response to

Harry and Kiley that I was looking for! I took a deep breath, got everyone's attention, and—aiming for a calm, yet serious tone—said, "I want to tell you all something very important. At Pacific Primary, you can be whatever you want to be.

At our school, you can celebrate whatever you want to celebrate, no matter what your hair looks like, how tall or short you are, or what color your skin is.

Celebrations are important in many families. Harry is telling us how important tonight is for him and his family. Harry, tell us more. Tell us about the apples and honey!"

Harry's big smile returned to his beautiful face. He jumped back into telling us about the celebration he so anticipated with his family. The children at the table, including Kiley, listened to Harry intently. Harry enthusiastically suggested, "Maybe my Mom can come and bring apples and honey for everyone! She can read my books, too!"

"Oh no!" Kiley exclaimed. "I hope it's not tomorrow! I'll be in Tahoe and I'll miss it! Harry, can you please save me the books and the apples and honey?!"

"Sure, Kiley, I'll save the books and even some apples and honey!" Harry assured her. The shift in their conversation was such a reminder that children seem to navigate these waters more easily than we adults do.

While I was not sure if my response was spot-on, I felt confident that what I said gave all of us a foothold in a rough patch, and would be a point of reference in the future. Most importantly, I felt sure that Harry would go home excited instead of diminished.

I've heard that disequilibrium is a springboard for new learning; it sure was for me. I came away from this conversation unsettled and full of questions. All of those voices that had offered their perspectives during that long moment when time stopped deserved to be revisited. They had raised big questions for me to consider.

- *How do I bring my full self—a Latina raised by immigrant parents, in a predominantly White community—to my teaching?*

- *What do I think about my sister's rules? Had I been using those rules when I'd redirected rather than engaged conversations like this in the past?*

- *How are children thinking about race and racism, and what is my responsibility to them?*

- *What about my colleagues' perspectives about keeping children safe from the violence of segregation and racism?*

- *What is my role as a teacher?*

- *How am I going to bravely work my way through these questions, moving forward from here? How will I be safe, secure, and supported as I continue my journey as an anti-bias educator?*

What Next?

I knew I had to think with other people about what had happened—needed to have real conversations, not just the swirl of voices that had surfaced at the lunch table. I wrestled with self-doubts. *Had I responded in the best way? What would my site director, Lynn, say? Being a White woman, would she be able to relate to how I was feeling? Was I over-reacting? Making a big deal out of "kids just being kids"? Should I first confide in another teacher of color? Should I tell the children's families about what had happened? How? What might they think of me as their children's teacher?*

Seeking Guidance from My Site Director, Lynn

After lunch, I went to my site director's office to let her know about the apples and honey conversation. I wanted to talk with Lynn because I needed some reassurance that I had done the right thing—and some help in processing what had happened. *Could I have used this opportunity in a different way? Had I said too much, or too little about race?* In our ten years of working together, Lynn and I had often collaborated in working through challenging situations with children and families. I trusted her to help me think through the conversation with Harry and Kiley.

Lynn listened to the story; her response encouraged me: "I'm glad you spoke directly to the issue of difference," she said. Although race and religion could be a tricky topic with young children, we were on the same page about supporting young children's capacity to sort through their questions and confusions about how people are alike and different, and the meaning of the differences between people. I asked Lynn if I ought to call Kiley's and Harry's parents to let them know about the lunchtime conversation (to be honest, I secretly hoped that Lynn would offer to call, but no luck). She encouraged me to get on the phone with the two families. I gulped, and holding onto the boost of confidence that my conversation with Lynn had given me, turned to the phone.

Making the Call

Even though it was only the third week of school, I already felt a strong connection with Harry's mom, Alexis; she was easy to talk with, and I admired her kind, warm interactions with Harry. And, as a mom of mixed-race kids myself, I related to Harry's racially and culturally-mixed family: Alexis is a White Jewish woman, and Harry's dad, Nick, is Black with Jamaican heritage.

I decided to call Alexis first. I hoped that a conversation about this achy experience for Harry would help us build a strong relationship, but still, my heart raced as I made the call. Harry had been on the receiving end of a really hurtful comment. *How would Alexis receive the news? What would she think about my response?* As a mom of mixed-race children, this was a call I wouldn't want to get.

I told Alexis about how excited Harry was about celebrating Rosh Hashanah. Then came the hard part. I described Kiley's response (though I didn't identify her by name, in the interest of confidentiality). Alexis took a long, audible breath before responding. Much of our conversation is a blur to me now; my head was spinning with everything that had happened that day for the children—and for me. What stood out the most was Alexis saying, "This is my worst fear for my brown babies." I could tell by the sound of her voice that she was trying not to cry. My eyes teared up, too, as I felt her ache, and our shared dismay that we need to worry about our children being excluded and treated unfairly because of the color of their skin, even in preschool.

Our phone call was a short one, perhaps because it was such a difficult conversation to have. Maybe we were both in shock that an-excited-to-share Harry had this experience. As adults who cared deeply about that eager guy, we, too, felt vulnerable. This was the first of a series of courageous conversations we would have, and we began well together. We listened to each other and spoke frankly, with open hearts.

We followed our phone call with an email exchange that included Nick, Harry's dad.

Email from Alexis:

I had the initial anxiety I always get when I see a call come through from school, but you re-assured me right away that Harry was safe and ok, so I relaxed. As you told me what had happened, my eyes filled with tears. When you said that Harry looked confused and hurt by the other child's comments, I was stuck on what his face looks like when he is confused and hurt. I could see it in my mind and it made me so sad. I know it's cliché, but I do feel part of my heart lives outside of me since having children and up until this point it had mostly been filled with joy and wonder watching him grow. This was a moment when it broke a little and I felt powerless to protect him from the world.

The other thought I had was I can't believe this is happening already. I am not naive and know that we live in a world where the color of your skin matters and that he would face racist and other-ing comments. I just did not expect it yet. So, overall I felt very sad and a little mad. I will admit I was angry that it happened, not at the other child in particular but at the world and the fact that it is this way. I also felt grateful to be in a place like Pacific Primary where we are lucky enough to have a skilled teacher to recognize the impact of such a moment and facilitate it. ~Alexis

Email from Nick:

Nadia, after hearing what had happened to Harry at school, I felt very sad that he had to experience something like this so young in a place that normally feels so totally safe. It made me think about the first time that someone explicitly told me that I could not do something because I am Black (which was when I was six). I also felt grateful that he was at a place like Pacific Primary that works so hard to help kids to value difference and I am determined to reassure him and support him in whatever way I can. ~Nick

I was honored by Nick's and Alexis's willingness to share their vulnerable worry, and at the same time, I wanted to reassure them that although Kiley's comment was hurtful, I did not think her intention was to hurt or exclude Harry.

I reaffirmed to them how important it was to me that their family felt safe at school, and alongside our directors and my teaching team, I would be proactive in helping guide the children's thinking about diversity, inclusion, religion, and race. I felt that a good place to start was to learn about Rosh Hashanah. I invited Alexis to visit our classroom to share her family's Rosh Hashanah traditions; we made plans for her to come to circle time the next day to read Harry's books about Rosh Hashanah—and, of course, to bring apples and honey!

Another Hard Call

After phoning Alexis, I called Kiley's dad, Mark. I had butterflies in my stomach: this was as hard as calling Harry's mom, though in a different way. *How could Kiley's dad and I talk about this in a way that wasn't about Kiley being "bad" or a budding racist?* I didn't want to make too big a deal about this, but at the same time, it *was* a big deal. *And what about Kiley's comment invoking her dad's authority on the subject of who can celebrate Rosh Hashanah? Perhaps she just said that to add credibility to what she was saying?* I didn't want Mark to think that I believed he'd actually told her, "Only people with white skin can celebrate" the holiday—I really didn't want to even go there, to be honest. *But how would I respond if I sensed we had different values? What if he disapproved of how I responded to the children?* I reminded myself that communication is the cornerstone to any sort of genuine collaboration with families—and that frank communication can feel vulnerable and exposed. So, I dug deep for courage and called Mark (I chose not to tell him who Kiley had directed her comments to).

Mark's immediate, astounded response was, "I am so sorry! I don't know where Kiley got that idea!" I could hear his embarrassment and worry.

Even as Mark fumbled for words, I assured him that I didn't judge him or Kiley—but that I did want us to take this seriously as something to figure out together. Mark wanted to understand where Kiley's statement came from: he had never heard her say anything like that and was shocked by her comment. "We don't really talk about race at home," he said. I explained my understandings that children are influenced by what they see around them and Kiley was just pointing out what she knew about her own experience of being Jewish. Mark gulped, saying, "I see now that Kiley has ideas about race and religion that we didn't know she had. Her mom and I need to take a more active role in discussing these big topics with her."

"I'm not an expert at how to handle comments like this," I responded. "But I am passionate about supporting children to see difference as a good thing." I shared my hope that by thinking together with both children's families, I'd strengthen my skills at responding to loaded moments like the lunchtime conversation. We went on to discuss how we could use this experience to support Kiley's learning—and our own.

Throughout our conversation, I was moved by Mark's thoughtfulness and self-reflection. He asked about the other child, saying that he felt terrible for him, and really regretted that Kiley's words had made him feel excluded and separated from the other kids.

As we hung up, Mark was reassuringly grateful that I'd called. And right away, he sent me a follow-up email of appreciation. I was relieved and hopeful to be launched on a course of honest dialogue. We made a plan to meet with Lynn, our site director, after Kiley's mom, Sarah, and Mark had a chance to talk together. Our meeting would give us a chance to figure out, together, how best to support Kiley and the rest of the children in their emerging understandings of race, religion, commonalities, and differences.

Being Brave

While relieved at the responses I was getting from both children's families, I continued to feel the unsettledness of being in new terrain. As I anticipated the meeting with Mark, Sarah, and Lynn, I knew it would not be a typical parent meeting; I had never had a meeting with parents about race and racism. I was acutely aware that I would be the only person of color at this meeting. I guessed that none of the other folks at the meeting knew what it felt like to be excluded or feel dismissed or diminished because of the color of their skin. I would bring a unique lens to our conversation as a Latina woman. I was not sure if I was ready to share my experience of those raw and vulnerable feelings. What I was sure about was that I was committed to being brave and participating in this meeting as fully as I could, no matter how uncomfortable we would all be feeling. I wanted to understand Mark's and Sarah's and Lynn's perspectives, and to share my ideas about how to think with Kiley about race, religion, and diversity.

As our meeting approached, I wondered how Mark and Sarah were feeling. *Were they embarrassed or disturbed, thinking their child's hurtful comment was a reflection of their parenting?* Perhaps they were as nervous as I was. I admired their courageousness. Because they were staying in contact, I was confident that even though we had different life experiences, we would think well together about how to support Kiley.

Wow, was I right! Mark began our meeting by telling us that they'd learned from Kiley that Harry was the person she'd talked to about Rosh Hashanah—and he and Sarah had called Harry's parents to apologize, and invited them to their home to celebrate Rosh Hashanah together. Harry's family had accepted the offer and they had spent the weekend together sharing Jewish New Year.

Now it was my turn to be stunned! Stunned—and deeply moved. I was tearful and my heart was filled with joy as Mark and Sarah told us about their weekend with Alexis, Nick, and Harry. They'd been wonderfully proactive in showing Harry's family that they cared about Harry's experience. They were ready to take this difficult situation head on and turn it into a positive learning experience for Kiley—and for themselves.

And Alexis and Nick had been beautifully responsive. They'd bravely listened to Kiley's parents, and accepted their invitation to celebrate together, changing their usual holiday plans in order to embrace this opportunity for connection. I felt a renewed hope for the possibilities of living with curiosity, peace, and respect in our troubled world.

This generous act of trust and connection between these two families set the stage for the next part of our meeting. We turned our attention to how to move forward.

How Children Learn about Identity and Difference

We expanded our conversation to consider how children learn about identity and difference. Children's brains are rapidly sorting and classifying, creating schema to understand the world.[2] As Mark and Sarah thought about how Kiley had come to her conclusion that only people with white skin can celebrate Rosh Hashanah, they recognized that there are no people of color at their temple. With the typical curious mind of an observant child, Kiley had certainly noticed this, and drawn her own conclusions about who can be Jewish and what Jewish people look like. This was sure a strong reminder to all of us that we adults have to be intentional about what we expose children to in their everyday lives as children form their understanding of "normal," and "right and wrong."

As we talked, I emphasized that our classroom conversation about diversity would not be a one-time thing, but ongoing. And Mark and Sarah were ready to set a course at home to actively engage a conversation about racial differences and religion. Lynn and I shared ways that they could navigate these big topics. We suggested that first they should follow

To continue to provoke conversations about skin color differences, I invited children to play a game with me: "Let's all put our hands in a circle and see what's the same and different about them."

Kiley's lead and honestly explore what she was wondering: "Are all Jewish people White?" *How might they help her discover why she thought that?* Understanding how she came to her theory about who can be Jewish would help them guide her to new understandings.

To help them call out Kiley's confusions, we framed some entry points that Mark and Sarah might use: "It's true that all the people at our temple have white skin. But learning that Harry is Jewish and that he has brown skin reminds us that many different kinds of people can be Jewish. Religion and race are different ideas."

The list that Mark, Sarah, and I created helped us choose books to read and talk about with the children.

Our role as adults, we agreed, is to offer comments and questions that tease out the tangles in children's thinking to help them develop more complex understandings.

Lynn, Sarah, Mark, and I turned to Piaget's cognitive development theory to remind ourselves that children go through different stages of understanding.[3]

These include:
- noticing the attributes of things;
- noticing how things are the same and different;
- noticing the characteristics that something does or does not possess;
- holding more than one attribute in mind at a time;
- distinguishing between "some" and "all."

Building on Piaget's theory, we can guide children to notice all the characteristics that one person, family, or object has, which supports the development of the disposition to avoid simple conclusions and to think more complexly. A car can be red, but are all cars red? A White person can be Jewish, but are all Jewish people White? Are all White people Jewish? We thought about how we could nudge this sort of thinking for Kiley at home, and for all the children at school.

I suggested literature as a way to introduce Kiley and the other children to a range of people, and to acknowledge that all of us are "different" in some way. I was reminded of the work of Bishop and shared his notion that children's books can serve as both mirrors and windows to offer views of the world around us, both imaginary and in our real physical world.[4] We started a list of books that Mark and Sarah could use at home and that I could use at school.

We also made plans for other action that I would take in the classroom. I would invite all of the families in our group to do a "family share," by visiting our classroom to offer their religious and cultural traditions and celebrations, their favorite books, their family recipes. And I would bring books to the classroom to help us think about, understand, and celebrate differences; we'd read and discuss these books in small groups.

We would emphasize with the children: "You know you best. Be proud of who you are!"[5] To underscore this message, we'd invite each of the children to create an art piece to capture what delighted them about themselves. We left our meeting with plans for home and school, ready to work with the children on this offering they had given us. This was different than any other parent or curriculum meeting I had experienced: we were all embarking into unfamiliar territory.

We invited each of the children to create an art piece to capture what delighted them about themselves.

Experiencing the Value of Collaboration

What good fortune to have gone through this experience with Harry's and Kiley's families! We had not expected—nor were we necessarily ready for—such a deep exploration so early in our time together. Yet this difficult situation brought us together intimately and immediately, planting the seeds for relationships rooted in trust, respect, vulnerability, and uncertainty. For most of us, race and religion are not mealtime conversations, especially not in the first weeks of a new relationship! But here we were—children, teachers, and families—in a deep dive together launched by a casual, powerful comment over lunch.

Typically, when parents get a phone call from school, it is about a scrape on their child's knee or a bump on their head. I am sure that when the school's number appeared on Alexis's and Mark's phone screens, they didn't expect to hear this story. But from the get-go, our conversations were open and honest and courageous. There was no defensiveness, no sugarcoating, or backpedaling. I felt able to tell the families that I was not an expert at talking to children about race and racism, and that this was new work I was undertaking.

Alexis opened her heart, describing how scary it was for her to learn that her child had been excluded because of the color of his skin. Mark was willing to share that his family hadn't talked overtly about race. In our conversations, we talked with open hearts; we learned about our differences and discovered our shared values about supporting children to see and honor diversity and inclusiveness. Together, in this collaborative stance, we learned how to listen to the children and how to respond to their curiosities, no matter how challenging or uncomfortable they were.

My initial hesitation and fear gave way to exhilaration and to new trust and confidence in myself. I wanted to call my sister and tell her what happened when I broke two of her conversation rules, to convey to her the fellowship that can emerge when we are willing to be vulnerable, to share our values and fears, and listen with curiosity.

"And the day
came when the risk
to remain tight in
a bud was more
painful than the risk
it took to blossom."

–Anais Nin

Chapter Two
Conversations Deepen

In the days that followed the lunchtime conversation, and after my initial exchanges with Harry's and Kiley's folks, I recognized that I needed the support of a thinking partner in order to provide thoughtful leadership in this emerging exploration of identity. I especially needed to talk with a person of color, someone who could relate to what I was experiencing, and who shared with me the experience of living with systemic racism.

I turned to Eric, another teacher at Pacific Primary. He had been Harry's teacher when Harry was two, and we'd talked at other times about the connection he felt with Harry. Both of them are multi-racial, with a Black father and a White, Jewish mother. "Harry reminds me of myself as a young child," Eric had mentioned once to me. "When I met his grandmother from Florida, I told Harry, 'I have a Bubbe, too, just like you.'" Eric seemed the perfect person for me to think—and to feel—with.

I sat with Eric in the staff lounge and spilled out the story of the lunchtime conversation, my first calls to Harry's and Kiley's parents, and my swirl of emotions and uncertainties. Eric's response caught me by surprise. "I'm coming to your classroom for morning meeting! I want to share my experience growing up and how kids did not believe I was Jewish because of the way I looked." Eric and I had been friendly co-workers for almost ten years, but this was the first time he had offered to come to my classroom for a morning meeting. Delighted and touched, I accepted—even though I felt a bit protective of Eric. Race is hard to talk about outside of your own identity group, let alone be vulnerable in front of four- and five-year-olds who see you as a revered teacher. When Eric came to morning meeting, he brought a photo of Dr. Martin Luther King Jr. marching with a rabbi. He knew that the children knew of Dr. King and looked up to him; the photo of Dr. King with a rabbi was a striking visual representation of friendship across differences. Eric used the photo to introduce the story of his life as a dark-skinned Jewish man. He told us about his childhood, how Harry's family reminded him a lot of his family, and how people didn't believe he was Jewish because of how he looks.

Rabbi Abraham Heschel presents a Judaism and World Peace award to Dr. Martin Luther King Jr.

© Library of Congress

Teacher Eric sharing at morning meeting (above). Teacher Lucia talking about her experience working at a Jewish Preschool (below).

As Eric talked, Harry's face lit up. He whispered to his friends sitting next to him, "That happened to me!" Harry made eye contact with other kids, as if to say, "Hey, Eric's like me! It's what we've been talking about—it's my story!" And Kiley, too, seemed happy to have her and Harry's experience carried into another story. Eric's visit was a generous gift to the children, and to me: the gift of talking frankly and bravely about identity, difference, and acceptance.

As other teachers at our school learned about Eric's visit to my group, they offered to share their own stories about their cultural traditions. Eric's generous gesture of support and sharing had sown the seeds for a deeper level of collaboration among our staff. I felt our staff stepping into new terrain as we began to talk about our cultural and racial contexts with each other, and with the children.

Growing Our Curriculum and Community

I emailed Harry's parents the day after Eric's visit:

Hi Alexis and Nick, I wanted to let you know that Teacher Eric came to our morning meeting yesterday to tell us stories about when he was a child and about Jewish celebrations he shared with his mom. Eric also shared that his family looks a lot like Harry's. Harry was very excited that Eric made this connection known in front of his peers. He was very proud! How is Harry doing at home? Sincerely, Nadia

Alexis responded:

Hi Nadia, Thank you so much for this email; it warmed our hearts. Harry brings us so much love and joy and I am glad he is free to share himself with the classroom. I thought I couldn't love Teacher Eric more and, of course, now I do. We are so grateful to you and the Pacific Primary community for seeing Harry, lifting him up and helping us all navigate difference. Harry is doing well at home; we struggle at times with negotiating the brewing sibling stuff, but he always amazes us with his kindness and capacity to talk through things. Have a great weekend. Best, Alexis

Other parents began hearing about this emergent, sensitive work, which we began to understand as our "curriculum."

It seemed time for expanded, purposeful communications with all of our classroom families.

Using Learning Stories as an Invitation to Collaborate

An important part of how we grow our curriculum is through studying our documentation—our notes and photos about the life we share with children in the classroom. We use the format of Learning Stories adapted from the approach to documentation and formative assessment developed in Aotearoa New Zealand.[6]

Typically, a Learning Story is written to a child, describing an experience or conversation that teachers observe and why it seems significant. We've discovered that Learning Stories contribute to children's identity development and strengthen the web of relationships in our community. We write Learning Stories for ourselves, to help us think more deeply about children's experiences and the significance of what's unfolding for children—why these moments matter. We share the Learning Stories with children, as invitations for them to reflect on their experiences. And we offer Learning Stories to families, which creates opportunities to connect in a meaningful way.

The focus of our Learning Stories varies, but we try to show families how ordinary moments with children can be quite extraordinary. Indeed, teachers often rediscover this ourselves, as we make meaning of the details of children's play and conversations. We've been using the Thinking Lens© protocol for this deeper reflection and meaning making, considering other perspectives, and possible next steps we might take in light of what we value and the responses we get from families.[7]

I decided to write a Learning Story about Apples and Honey—the conversation over lunch, and the conversations with the families (and with Eric) that followed. I was proud about the expanding circles of collaboration and the ways in which the collaboration was shaping our curriculum. In the Learning Story, I hoped to share not only what we were doing, but how we were challenged, and what we were learning about ourselves; I was eager for families to see the positive outcomes available to us when adults directly engage children's ideas about difference. I also wanted to prompt families to initiate these conversations with their children at home—and, I hoped, to talk with me and my co-teachers about their values and ideas about how we could continue to talk about difference at school.

I realized that this was going to be hard for me to write; this was the first time that I—or anyone at our school—had written a learning story about race and religion. I wanted to respect both families' privacy. And, especially with Kiley's family, I worried that they might feel embarrassed or ashamed. I wanted to share my personal reflections, but I worried that the families and educators at our school might not be ready to hear what I had to say.

I decided that I would focus my learning story on the children's lunchtime exchange about who can and can't celebrate Shana Tova, and on my response. I hoped that this would be a starting point for a larger conversation about race, racism, and religious diversity. I checked in with Harry's and Kiley's families, to get their thumbs up to share this version of the tender story about their children, then I posted the Apples and Honey Learning Story.

Learning Story

Apples & Honey

Author: Nadia Jaboneta
Coyote Classroom
October 9, 2017

It was a sunny day at Pacific Primary and in the Coyote Classroom, we were enjoying a delicious lunch together. The children and teachers were engaged in meaningful conversations about our day. Harry began to tell us about his evening plans: "I'm so excited for tonight! I'm going to celebrate Shana Tova! I'm going to eat apples and honey, and my Mom is going to read me my books about the celebration!"

Harry's excitement was contagious! Children asked him questions about this celebration and Harry had detailed responses. A question came up about who can and can't celebrate Shana Tova based on what they look like, with one child declaring that only White people can celebrate Rosh Hashanah. I knew that I needed to say something to challenge that biased understanding, and to support Harry in his excited pride about his family's celebration.

Learning Story

I got everyone's attention at our table and responded, "At Pacific Primary, you can be whatever you want to be. At Pacific Primary, you can celebrate whatever you want to celebrate, no matter what your hair looks like, how tall or short you are or what color your skin is. Celebrations are important in many families." I then invited Harry to continue telling us about this wonderful celebration with his family. "Maybe my Mom can come and bring apples and honey for everyone!" Harry exclaimed. "She can read my books, too!"

Learning Story

Later that day, Alexis (Harry's mom) and I made plans to have a circle time in the classroom where she would read Harry's books about Rosh Hashanah and other Jewish holidays, and of course, share apples and honey! We made this plan as a way to expand children's anti-bias understandings, and to bring to life what I'd said during lunch: families of all skin colors celebrate religious holidays, including Rosh Hashanah.

Coyote kids, I am looking forward to thinking together about the important role that celebrations have in our lives and in our community. I am excited to learn with you about how people who look different from each other share celebrations, and how people who look the same as each other celebrate different holidays.

In the Coyote classroom, we value celebrating diversity, traditions, and holidays. Educators and parents have learned that, between the ages of three and five, children begin to develop stereotypes about themselves and others. Children are influenced by everything that they see around them (television, books, advertisements, adult behavior, etc.). As the adults in these children's lives, it is our responsibility to help children respect each other, themselves, and all people.

Learning Story

We can use spontaneous moments as opportunities for learning, such as in the conversation about Rosh Hashanah in the story above. We can also be proactive and help guide the children's thinking, challenging the stereotypes that they are at risk of internalizing, and instilling curiosity about and appreciation for differences.

Inspired by Harry's enthusiasm and pride about his family celebration of Rosh Hashanah, the Coyote Teaching Team invites you to share your family celebrations and traditions with us. This is an opportunity to help broaden the children's awareness of their own and others' cultural experiences. This is also a wonderful way to build relationships and support our ongoing curriculum of "Love is a Family."

> **"At Pacific Primary, you can be whatever you want to be. At Pacific Primary, you can celebrate whatever you want to celebrate, no matter what your hair looks like, how tall or short you are or what color your skin is."**
>
> *–Quote inspired by*
> *Daniel Gill and Keiko Shimozaki*

Learning Story

**Anti-Bias Education Goals
Derman-Sparks & Edwards, 2010**

Goal #1: Identity
> Each child will demonstrate self-awareness, confidence, family pride, and positive social/group identities.

Goal #2: Diversity
> Each child will express comfort and joy with human diversity, accurate language for human differences, and deep, caring human connections.

Goal #3: Justice
> Each child will increasingly recognize unfairness (injustice), have language to describe unfairness, and understand that unfairness hurts.

Goal #4: Activism
> Each child will demonstrate a sense of empowerment and the skills to act, with others or alone, against prejudice and/or discriminatory actions.

To extend children's thinking about family identity and culture, we read the book, <u>Who's in a Family?</u> by Robert Skutch. Then, we invited the children to draw portraits of their families to share with each other.

Seeking Common Ground in Our Different Perspectives

As I wrote the Apples and Honey Learning Story, I heard the echo of many voices that had reverberated in my head through that long, slow moment at the lunch table after Kiley's exclamation to Harry. How might each of these people in my life read the Learning Story, I wondered? I decided to use the story to circle back to one of those voices.

I emailed the Learning Story to Belann, our school's Executive Director. I value her perspective, and hoped we could continue the conversation that we'd begun several years ago at the meeting about anti-bias books and whether it was appropriate to introduce stories of racism, segregation, and injustice to young children. Giving Belann the Apples and Honey Learning Story would launch us, I hoped, into a courageous conversation—one in which we risked the possibility of awkwardness and discomfort in order to deepen our understandings of each other's perspectives, values, and convictions. I believed that we shared a commitment to doing right by children. *But*, I thought, our ideas about what that meant had some overlap and some divergence.

We shared the anti-bias goal of supporting children to develop the ability to confidently and empathetically explore differences, but we had divergent ideas about when and how we ought to talk with children about race and racism.[8] Offering my Learning Story to Belann would be a way to learn more about her thinking, and to offer her an expanded picture of mine. I feel it is important to be pro-active in addressing anti-bias goals by creating a safe space for children to have honest conversations—with a trusted teacher—about how racism serves to exclude people because of the color of their skin.

I sent my Learning Story off to Belann, and waited for a response. What I heard from her energized me:
Spectacular! What a beautiful and moving learning story. I will share with all of our teachers as I know it will inspire them too.

With Belann's affirmation, I felt ready for more collaboration with the families and teachers. I also wanted to research more about how young children perceive race and racism, and explore how we, as important adults in their lives, can support them with healthy identity development and unseat fear of differences among people. I was curious to find ways we might continue to learn together as a staff, moving from the first step Belann suggested of sharing the Apples and Honey Learning Story.

**Belann did send the Learning Story
to the full staff, with a note:**

Please read this excellent learning story from Nadia
that highlights how to include diverse celebrations in
your classroom.

It also shows how confidently she handled a potentially
awkward situation when a child in the classroom told
the children that Harry could not celebrate a Jewish
holiday because of his skin color. She spoke to both sets
of parents and they felt very grateful for how she
addressed this situation.

And Belann followed that with an invitation to me and my
colleague, Brian, to share with our staff the presentation
about anti-bias curriculum that we'd recently presented
at a local conference. I'd hoped to move forward with
deeper collaboration with my co-workers—and here was
the opportunity. I didn't have to think twice before accepting
Belann's invitation! My excitement took a dip when Brian
contracted the flu; however, when Belann suggested that
we could reschedule our presentation, I knew I needed to
carry on and go solo as the workshop leader.

Chapter Two: Conversations Deepen

"*Vulnerability sounds like truth and feels like courage. Truth and courage aren't always comfortable, but they're never weakness.*"

–Bréne Brown

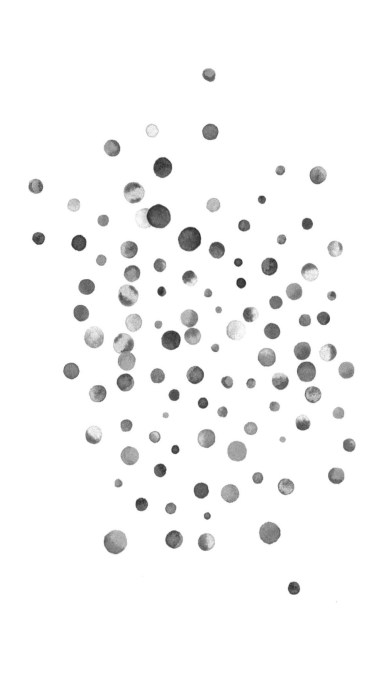

Chapter Three

Courage Guides

It seemed fitting to launch my presentation to our staff with the story that was most immediately connected with my learning about anti-bias practices. I began the workshop with the story of Harry's and Kiley's exchange over lunch, and with my conversations with their families. Then, to validate the importance of anti-bias learning, I put up a slide: "They're not too young to talk about race," with a chart offered by Jarrod Green that summed up research that demonstrates that silence about race reinforces racism.[9]

As I reviewed the information on the slide, I anticipated strong responses from my colleagues. But there was quiet in the room, until a teacher of color offered an aching and tender story about her own child's experience of being excluded and treated differently at school because of the color of her skin. "Why did you not tell Kiley that her words about Harry's skin color were hurtful?" she asked poignantly. This was the moment I'd dreaded and anticipated, this moment of diving deep and authentically into shared reflection.

I wanted to answer honestly, neither defensive nor brashly self-assured. And I wanted my response to generate further discussion, not silence it. I'd been longing for this sort of raw and real exploration, hungry to continue my learning with my colleagues. And so, I answered honestly and simply: "I agree that what Kiley said *was* hurtful, but in that

They're not too young to talk about race!

0	1	2	3	4	5	6+
At birth, babies look equally at faces of all races. At 3 months, babies look more at faces that match the race of their caregivers. (Kelly et al. 2005)	Children as young as two years use race to reason about people's behaviors. (Hirschfeld, 2008)	By 30 months, most children use race to choose playmates. (Katz & Kofkin, 1997)	Expressions of racial prejudice often peak at ages 4 and 5. (Aboud, 2008)	By five, Black and Latinx children in research settings show no preference toward their own groups compared to Whites; White children at this age remain strongly biased in favor of whiteness. (Dunham et al. 2008)	By kindergarten, children show many of the same racial attitudes that adults in our culture hold—they have already learned to associate some groups with higher status than others. (Kinzler, 2016)	Explicit conversations with 5–7 year olds about interracial friendship can dramatically improve their racial attitudes in as little as a single week. (Bronson & Merryman, 2009)

Young children notice and think about race. Adults often worry that talking about race will encourage racial bias in children, but the opposite is true. **Silence about race reinforces racism** by letting children draw their own conclusions based on what they see. Teachers and families can play a powerful role in helping children of all ages develop positive attitudes about race and diversity and skills to promote a more just future—but only if we talk about it!

Do some learning of your own to get ready for conversations with children. Here are some good places to seek *information* and *training*:
- Teaching Tolerance — tolerance.org
- Raising Race Conscious Children — raceconscious.org
- Embrace Race — embracerace.org
- Teaching for Change — teachingforchange.org
- AORTA Cooperative — aorta.coop
- Fortify Community Health (CA) — fortifycommunityhealth@gmail.com
- Delaware Valley Assoc. for the Education of Young Children (PA) — dvaeyc.org

© 2018 • Updated Feb 26 2018
The Children's Community School
1212 South 47th Street, Philadelphia PA 19143
childrenscommunityschool.org

Infographic created by the Children's Community School, based in part on information and ideas from Jillian Addler at First Up, Lori Riddick at Raising Race Conscious Children, and kiran nigam at Anti-Oppression Resource and Training Alliance (AORTA).

moment, I did not want her to feel ashamed for sharing her ideas. Also, I felt cautious about tackling her comments head-on, because I knew that some people on our staff are concerned that it's not appropriate to take up the complex topic of racism with young children."

At that, Belann stood up and exclaimed, "I've been one of those people. But I think we have more learning to do about this. I want to propose that we form a group of teachers who want to study this further with me. I want to think more about how we should approach conversations about race and racism with young children."

What a powerful moment this was for me! I'd been on a teeter-totter of nerves and excitement heading into the workshop. And now, the nerves gave way to full-on gratitude for our staff. We were embarking on the course that I'd hoped for: thinking as a staff about talking about racial identity, and finding sensitive ways to acknowledge racism and the real impact it has on people, and our school's commitment to justice and change. I couldn't wait to call Brian, home sick: this would be a tonic for his flu!

Final Reflections: Discovering Who I Am

As the year progressed, the children continued to ponder questions of race and religion. It was a year-long seminar in anti-bias teaching, led by the four- and five-year-old children in my class! In the past, I would have sidestepped or squirmed away from these questions. Now, I was ready to wade in.

We are living in a time where the sentiments and meanness of racism have been fully unleashed. While I was growing up, my mom—an immigrant from Peru and a proud American citizen—often urged us to "Fight for your rights!" Her self-confidence and powerful stance were shaken this year when someone in the grocery store confronted her, telling her to "speak English and go back to your own country."

That experience only strengthened my desire to be a leader in this work. I see firsthand how racism infuses all of our lives, White people and people of color, children and adults. Since that moment at the lunch table, I've begun to listen for opportunities to take up the conversation about race and religion with the children as a way to plant the seeds for a more just society.

"My skin is a different color than my mom, but we are both Indian."

"Did you hear about what happened to Jesus?"

"You wouldn't know about Moses, because you're Jewish."

"Why is that boy wearing a dress?"

"That man in the store had a towel wrapped around his head."

"I saw this bad guy sleeping on the sidewalk!"

"Everybody here is chocolate except us."

To prepare myself for those moments when issues of race and religion surface in my classroom, I've crafted a set of questions to guide my response—questions that replaced the cacophony of voices that jostled for my attention at the lunch table with Harry and Kiley. I keep in mind questions like:

- *What touches my heart about this situation?*

- *What in my background or personal life is influencing my feeling and thinking right now?*

- *What might the children's families hope I'll say or do?*

- *How do my values about diversity and equity play into this situation?*

I feel new muscles developing, and I want to keep exercising them. One big change that I've made is how I write learning stories. I used to focus pretty narrowly on the story of what happened with the children and on the children's learning; now, I include a lot more of my own thinking and learning and questioning. I see learning stories as a way to deepen my collaboration with parents, sharing my learning with them and inviting them to help me deepen and expand my understandings and practice.

I now understand it's important to be pro-active in sparking conversations about race and religion—with both children and adults—rather than waiting for something hurtful to happen as a provocation for me to act. I'm also continuing to develop my understanding of core aspects of anti-bias learning.

Children's identity development can be infused with bias. Many things about how racism works are often invisible to people who are given privilege because of their skin color. Without White people even thinking about it or noticing it, people of color can become isolated and overlooked, if not directly silenced and oppressed.

People of color often internalize a "less than" mentality. White people internalize an identity of "normal" and assume that people who are different are "not as normal."

I'm a hungry learner, eager to fill in gaps in my understandings, to discover who shares my experience and what other experiences I need to know about. To seek out more perspectives from people of color, I've been watching numerous TED Talks. And reading, reading, reading. From Brené Brown, a White professor, author, and speaker, I've learned about the power of courage, vulnerability, and empathy.[10] From Deb Curtis, I've learned to really see children and to seek their perspectives.[11] This has brought alive the idea that "children have so much to teach us."

Inspired by signs they have seen in our community, the children wanted to make a sign for the entrance to our classroom.

I work in a remarkable school with a staff and administration that has not only allowed, but encouraged me to expand my thinking and leadership. The encouragement and concrete support of time for collaboration and resources to attend conferences and study tours have been a tremendous source of learning for me.

Sure, sometimes my heart still races or my mind freezes up when I find myself in a conversation about big topics, but I now have more confidence, courage, and knowledge to take on these conversations—with adults and children—no matter how hard or uncomfortable. Now I know I'll be able to respond when children say or ask something about what they notice.

There's a whole other level of challenge for me when co-workers and parents make a racist joke or speak from racist assumptions, or when they overlook the perspectives of people of color. Our community is progressive and thoughtful, but racism can make its way to the surface in ways that people often don't recognize. I'm learning to speak up in those moments, though my heart races.

When I've told people that I'm working on this book, so many folks have exclaimed, "I need to read that book and talk with other people about it!" I recognize in those comments a longing to be part of real and transformative conversations, to stop living fearfully and cautiously around people who are different. It grows from the big-hearted desire to live in what Dr. Martin Luther King Jr. called "the beloved community."[12]

Parents, grandparents, scout leaders, coaches, teachers, and all sorts of other people with children in our lives realize we need to create brave spaces to take up uncomfortable conversations.[13] The books and organizations centered around *Courageous Conversations* remind us that this is not only needed, but possible with valuable guides and protocols.[14]

We have to have these conversations across the identity lines that too often divide us. We can create inclusive and respectful cultures that honor differences. By learning and talking about our similarities and differences, about actions to counter unfairness, we are providing children with a strong foundation to create a different world, one brave, heartfelt conversation at a time! Or, as the children declared:

"We can spread kindness all over our neighborhood! All over San Francisco! All the way to the White House! All over the Universe! To Infinity!"

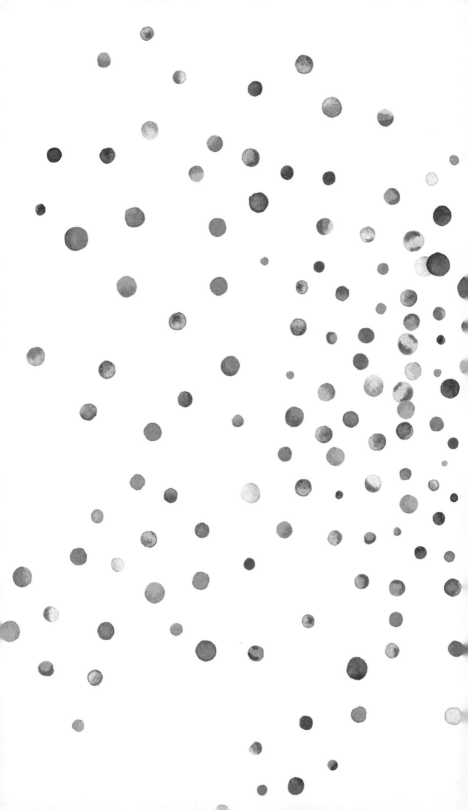

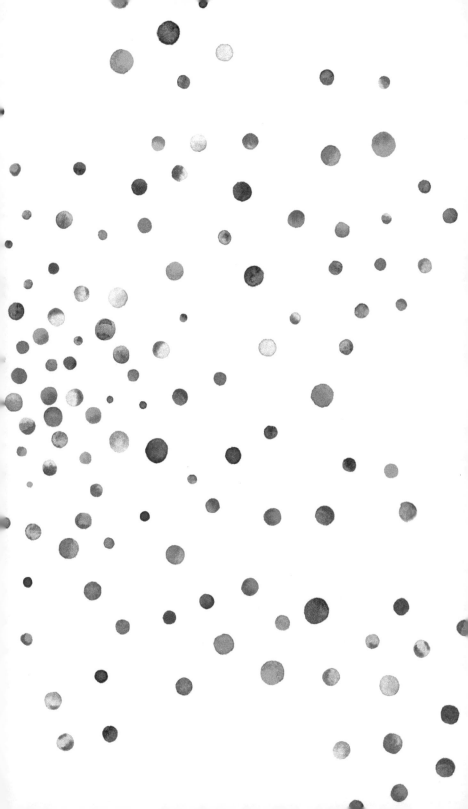

Notes

1   Jacqueline Woodson, *The Other Side* (New York: Penquin Young Readers Group, 2001).

2   Deb Curtis and Nadia Jaboneta, *Children's Lively Minds: Schema Theory Made Visible* (St. Paul: Redleaf Press, 2019).

3   Dorothy Singer and Tracey Revenson, *A Piaget Primer: How a Child Thinks* (New York: Penguin, 1996).

4   Rudine Sims Bishop, "Mirrors, Windows, and Sliding Glass Doors," *Perspectives: Choosing and Using Books for the Classroom* 6, no. 3 (Summer 1990), ix–xi.

5   Brook Pessin-Whedbee, *Who are You?: The Kid's Guide to Gender Identity* (London: Jessica Kingsley Publishers, 2017).

6   Margaret Carr and Wendy Lee, *Learning Stories: Constructing Learner Identities in Early Education* (Thousand Oaks: SAGE Publications, Inc., 2012).

7   The Thinking Lens© is an evolving protocol by Ann Pelo, Margie Carter, and Deb Curtis; the most recent version can be excerpted from: Ann Pelo and Margie Carter, *From Teaching to Thinking: A Pedagogy for Reimagining our Work* (Lincoln: Exchange Press, 2018).

8   Louise Derman Sparks and Julie Olsen Edwards, *Anti-Bias Education for Young Children and Ourselves*, 2d ed. (Washington D.C.: NAEYC, 2009).

9   "They're Not Too Young to Talk about Race," copyright © 2018 by the Children's Community School (childrenscommunityschool.org).

10   Brené Brown, *Dare to Lead: Brave Work. Tough Conversations. Whole Hearts.* (New York: Random House, 2018); *Daring Greatly: How the Courage to Be Vulnerable Transforms the Way We Live, Love, Parent, and Lead* (New York: Avery, 2015).

11   Deb Curtis, *Really Seeing Children* (Lincoln: Exchange Press, 2017).

12   Dr. Martin Luther King, Jr., *Where Do We Go From Here: Chaos or Community?* (Boston: Beacon Press, 1967).

13   Brian Arao and Kristi Clemens, "From Safe Spaces to Brave Spaces: A New Way to Frame Dialogue Around Diversity and Social Justice," in *The Art of Effective Facilitation* (Sterling: Sylus Publishing, 2013), 135-150.

14   Glenn Singleton, *Courageous Conversations about Race* (Thousand Oaks: Sage, 2015); Zaretta Hammond, *Culturally Responsive Teaching and the Brain: Promoting Authentic Engagement and Rigor Among Culturally and Linguistically Diverse Students* (Thousand Oaks: Corwin, 2014); Ijeoma Oluo, *So You Want to Talk About Race* (New York: Seal Press, 2018).

About the Author

Nadia Jaboneta is a program coordinator and classroom teacher at Pacific Primary preschool in San Francisco, California. She has 20 years of experience in the Early Childhood Education field teaching young children, training teachers, consulting, and facilitating workshops on reflective practice, social justice, project work, sensory integration, and schema theory. Nadia is proud to have immigrant parents from Lima, Peru. It is because of their hard work, resilience, and support that she is who she is today.

Nadia is one of the first people in her family to graduate from college here in the United States. She received her Bachelor's and Master's degrees from San Francisco State University where she concentrated on teacher research and the importance of capturing children's voices, as well as to reflect on her own practice. She is the co-author of *Children's Lively Minds: Schema Theory Made Visible* with Deb Curtis (St. Paul: Redleaf Press, 2019) as well as several articles in NAEYC's *Teaching Young Children* magazine.

Acknowledgments

Since I began my work as an Early Childhood Educator
20 years ago, I have loved telling stories about the amazing
things children say and do and what I learn from them.
Often, my colleagues and friends would say, "You should
write a book about that!" I honestly was not sure if that
would ever happen. Many years later, this dream was realized.
I am grateful for the encouragement and inspiration from
all of my ECE colleagues, mentors, and friends over the
years, including Sarah Johnson, Mia Cavalca, Daniel Meier,
and Barbara Henderson.

A special thanks to my dear friends and mentors Deb Curtis
and Margie Carter for listening to my stories and supporting
me in sharing the children's voices as well as my own.

I admire your dedication and commitment to working with professionals in the early childhood field. It is truly an honor to work with such extraordinary people. I have learned so much from both of you!

I am also thankful to Margie Carter for being my editor along with Ann Pelo. Working with both of you writing this book was an extremely rewarding experience and I could not have done it without you! You both showed such patience, brilliance, and motivation during this sometimes not so easy road of writing and sharing my social justice journey. I am grateful for our collaboration and for tirelessly working together to make this book what it is.

A big thank you to Emily Rose, Stacy Hawthorne and the rest of the amazing Exchange team that worked on this book and helped it come to life with its unique design. I appreciate your asking about my vision for this book and even the colors I would like! It was a wonderful experience collaborating with you.

My sincere thanks to my directors Belann Giarretto and Lynn Turner for their encouragement and help in making it possible for me to take this professional journey. I admire your passion in being social justice leaders and your courage in helping me share this story. Pacific Primary is such a special place and I feel lucky to be a part of this amazing community!

I would like to thank Brian Silveira for being an amazing friend, colleague, thinking partner, and incredible motivator in the work we have been doing together for the past 10 years. I am appreciative for your care, help, and guidance during this time of writing. I cannot imagine a world without team Bradia.

A big thank you to my teaching team Darby Hillyard and Riley Graham for always being onboard with going deeper into our curriculum, even when it was a little bit scary. I appreciate your patience and support as I took time off to write about the amazing work we are doing.

I am extremely grateful to the children and families involved in this story that I am sharing. Thank you for trusting me and thinking with me. You have all helped me get to know myself better and become a better teacher. The children give me hope for a better future!

Finally, I would like to thank my wonderful family for their continued love and support. Gracias familia! To my parents who have always wanted the best for me and taught me to work hard and "fight for my rights." To my sister for letting me include her in this story and for our daily morning phone calls. To my niece and nephew, thank you for being my first students and teaching me how important childhood is. Most importantly, to my daughters Ari and Leelah and my husband Jim for being there for me no matter what, and for your support and understanding during the countless hours I spent on my laptop. Thank you for helping me follow my dreams and for being social justice leaders along with me. I love you all to the moon and back!

From Reading to Thinking:
A Protocol for Reflection and Learning

You Can't Celebrate That! is a big story to take in, full of feeling, and vulnerability, and risk. As you read, you probably imagined yourself at the lunch table with Kiley and Harry, and gulped along with Nadia when Kiley made her bold declaration to Harry that "You can't celebrate [Rosh Hashanah]! Only people with white skin can celebrate that! That's what my Dad said." We know that the children in our care will make these sorts of unfiltered, sharp-edged statements—but when they do, we're startled and momentarily off-balance, unsure how to respond.

Nadia describes a chorus of voices in her head as she feels her way towards a response—her sister and Dad, her co-workers and supervisors, even aspects of her own identity make suggestions and offer challenges. Nadia's reflections serve as useful coaching for all of us to stay conscious of the perspectives, experiences, and relationships that shape our teaching. We are reminded to stay self-aware, to ask, "What ideas, voices, and assumptions might be influencing me, in moments like this?"

In the days following the conversation about Rosh Hashanah, Nadia continues to model self-awareness—and the courage to take emotional risks with parents, co-workers, and administrators. A masterful teacher, she recognizes her uncertainty about "the right" thing to do; in fact, she abandons the idea that there is _one_ right way, and, instead, focuses on cornerstone questions to guide her work—questions about her own learning, as well as the children's learning.

• _How do I bring my full self—a Latina raised by immigrant parents, in a predominantly White community—to my teaching?_

• _What do I think about my sister's rules? Had I been using those rules when I'd redirected rather than engaged conversations like this in the past?_

• _How are children thinking about race and racism, and what is my responsibility to them?_

• _What do I think about my colleagues' perspectives about keeping children safe from the violence of segregation and racism?_

Nadia's questions remind us that we do our best work as educators when we're asking questions of ourselves, rather than focusing solely on asking the children questions, or on our learning goals for them. Nadia is self-aware, and uncertain, and vulnerable in not-knowing—qualities of an educator (a human being!) committed to continued growth and evolution. To support her growth, Nadia seeks out people whose perspectives are different from her own; she turns to resources about child development and about social justice learning. She leans into her relationships with families, colleagues, and administrators. In all this, Nadia cultivates the discipline of lingering with uncertainty, and exploring questions with a multiplicity of answers.

A thinking protocol is a way to formalize the practice of asking questions to support reflective, responsive, relational teaching. To help you reflect on the significance of *You Can't Celebrate That!* for your teaching practice, we offer the following questions based on the Thinking Lens© protocol (as described in *From Teaching to Thinking: A Pedagogy for Reimagining Our Work*). The Thinking Lens© builds on the core principle of constructivism that people build their understandings through experience and reflection—in this case, through reading Nadia's story and reflecting on how it relates to your current teaching practices.

Using the signposts of the Thinking Lens©, these questions ask you to consider what moved you in *You Can't Celebrate That!*, what new perspectives you've gained, what actions you might take. Use these questions to help yourself articulate your learning, perhaps in writing, and then in conversation with colleagues and pedagogical companions.

Know yourself. Open your heart to this moment.
What touched you about this story?

In what ways did you see yourself and your experiences
in this story?

How were your values reflected in or challenged by
aspects of this story?

Take the children's points of view.
What are the children trying to figure out in their exchanges
about skin color, religious celebrations, and belonging?

What understandings, misunderstandings, and experiences
are the children drawing on?

Examine the environment.
What books, images, and people does Nadia bring into her
classroom? How might these support children's learning
about difference and identity? How might they continue to
deepen the conversation between Nadia, the children's
families, and her co-workers?

How would you describe the social and emotional
environments of this program?

How do these environments shape children's identities? Their confidence in having conversations about big ideas and questions?

Collaborate with others to expand perspectives.
What learning theories are you curious about after reading this story? How will you find out more about them?

As you discuss this book with others, how are your perspectives or ideas challenged?

What can you learn from this story about possibilities for talking with families about big issues? About collaborating with families to shape the curriculum of your classroom?

How does Nadia's courage with her co-workers and administrators inspire you to take up conversations about social justice issues in your program?

Reflect and take action.
Building on your reflections, write a statement that describes the learning that you will carry with you from *You Can't Celebrate That!*

What will you do differently in your work because of reading this book?

Reading a book is an investment of time and attention. To make the most of that investment, revisit sections of the book that engaged or confused you. Find study companions to help you reflect on *You Can't Celebrate That!*. Commit yourself to transforming your reading from a passive experience of listening to a good story to active engagement with thinking and questioning. Reading a book in this way becomes professional development.

May Nadia's story strengthen your capacity to take up conversations that matter, even when your heart thunders and your pulse races. May it encourage you to linger with uncertainty, and to seek out the many truths and perspectives at play in issues of social justice. May it sustain you in your work to carry kindness, generosity, and empathy into the community, the universe—to infinity!

—*Ann Pelo* and *Margie Carter*
Editors of the *Reimagining Our Work* (ROW) Collection

Authors of *From Teaching to Thinking: A Pedagogy for Reimagining Our Work*

"Every minute a chance to change the world..."

–Dolores Huerta

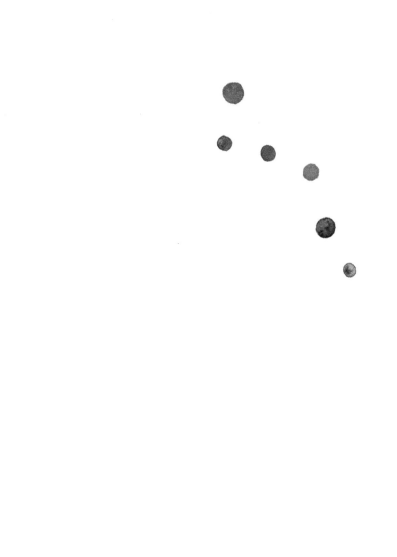